About This Book

Title: *Zip It, Snap It, Clip It!*

Step: 2

Word Count: 91

Skills in Focus: Consonant blends

Tricky Words: coat, snow, warm, heat, gloves, put, them

Ideas For Using This Book

Before Reading:
- **Comprehension:** Look at the title and cover image together. Walk through the pictures in the book with readers and have them make predictions about what they might learn in the book. Help them make connections by asking what they already know about warm clothes.
- **Accuracy:** Practice saying the tricky words listed on page 1.
- **Phonemic Awareness:** Explain to readers that a blend is two consonants together that each make a sound. Read aloud story words containing consonant blends, beginning with *sled*. Segment the sounds in the word slowly and have the students call out the word. Call attention to each blend and where it is found within the word. More consonant blend story words include *grab, must, slip, pants, snap, help,* and *stop*.

During Reading:
- Have readers point under each word as they read it.
- **Decoding:** If readers are stuck on a word, help them say each sound and blend the sounds together smoothly. You may want to point out consonant blends as they appear.
- **Comprehension:** Invite students to talk about what new things they are learning about warm clothes while reading. What are they learning that they didn't know before?

After Reading:
Discuss the book. Some ideas for questions:
- What is the weather like where you live? What clothes do you wear to stay comfortable?
- What items of clothing do you zip, snap, or clip?

Zip It, Snap It, Clip It!

Text by Marley Richmond

Reading Consultant
Deborah MacPhee, PhD
Professor, School of Teaching and Learning
Illinois State University

PICTURE WINDOW BOOKS
a capstone imprint

Let's sled! Grab a coat!

Kids must be warm.

Slip on socks.

Pull up snow pants.
Snow pants can be big.

Next, pull on a vest.
Zip it up.

Kids must put on coats.

A coat can zip.
It can snap.

Kids put on coats to help trap heat.

Stop! Not so fast.

Zip it, snap it!

A hat has flaps.

Its flaps help trap heat.

This hat cannot zip, snap, or clip.

Kids put on gloves.

Clip them on last!

In the cold, zip it, snap it, and clip it!

More Ideas:

Phonics and Phonemic Awareness Activity

Practicing Consonant Blends:
Play I Spy! Prepare word cards with consonant blend story words. Place each card face up on a surface. Choose a word to start the game. Say "I spy" and then segment the sounds in the word. For example, "I spy /s/, /l/, /e/, /d/." The readers will call out the word and then look for the corresponding card. Continue until all cards have been collected.

Suggested words:
- sled
- must
- stop
- soft

Extended Learning Activity

Play Pretend:
This book talks about warm clothes. Ask readers to pretend they are playing outside. What clothes might they need to wear to stay comfortable in the rain or in hot weather? Ask readers to explain how they zip, snap, or clip on their clothes. Challenge them to use words with consonant blends.

Published by Picture Window Books, an imprint of Capstone
1710 Roe Crest Drive, North Mankato, Minnesota 56003
capstonepub.com

Copyright © 2026 by Capstone.
All rights reserved. No part of this publication may be reproduced in whole or in part, or stored in a retrieval system, or transmitted in any form or by any means, electronic, mechanical, photocopying, recording, or otherwise, without written permission of the publisher.

Library of Congress Cataloging-in-Publication Data is available on the Library of Congress website.

ISBN: 9798875227011 (hardback)
ISBN: 9798875229459 (paperback)
ISBN: 9798875229435 (eBook PDF)

Image Credits: iStock: FatCamera, 5, Iryna Inshyna, 18–19, Iurii Krasilnikov, 22–23, kool99, 16, Tatiana Buzmakova, 7, 24, Wirestock, 1, 11; Shutterstock: Anna Mikhailovna, 6, Aynur_sib, 10, Fab_1, 8–9, JabaWeba, 17, simonovstas 2–3, Takayuki, 14–15, Tango007, 12–13, Tatyana Bakul, cover, Tetiana Bragina, 20, winnieapple, 4, yamasan0708, 21

Printed and bound in China. PO 6274